She Reveals When It's Time

*A Collection of Stories by
The Spiritual Journey Writers*

She Reveals When It's Time
Copyright © 2019 by Unity of Austin

All rights reserved.
Published in the United States of America. No part of this book may be reproduced or transmitted in any form or by any means, electronic or mechanical, including photocopying, recording, or by any information storage and retrieval system without the prior written permission of the Unity of Austin, except for the inclusion of brief quotations in critical reviews and certain other noncommercial uses permitted by copyright law. For permission requests or information, please contact the Unity of Austin

Photo of Spiritual Journey Writers by Dave Pedley

Published by
Positive Imaging, LLC
bill@positive-imaging.com
http://positive-imaging.com

ISBN: 9781944071943

All proceeds from the sale of this book benefit Unity of Austin, Austin, Texas.

Contents

	Foreword	7
	Letter to the Reader	9
	Dedication	11
I	Faith	13
II	Nature	27
III	Humanity	39
IV	Loss	43
V	Angels	49
VI	Intuition	59
VII	Grace - Reflection	67
VIII	Belief	77
IX	Love	95
X	Humor	103

Foreword
by Rev. Anna Shouse, Ph.D.
Senior Minister, Unity of Austin

Writing is by definition spiritual. The words that find their way onto the page emerge from one's inner life. On their passage to the surface they make what has been unknown known, what has been invisible visible. Writing is for the adventurous. It transforms. Writing reveals us to ourselves, and if we choose, to others. The Spiritual Journey Writers are a group of daring women who, gathering once a month here at Unity of Austin, dive their depths. They bring up treasures light, life, awareness. This collection of writings explores their finds expressed through themes of loss, love, angels, belief, nature, faith, grace, and reflection. Led by the group's founder Pastor Martha Iglehart, a deeply insightful author in her own right, the Spiritual Journey Writers are a rich consciousness of creativity and spirituality. We are fortunate that they have chosen to share their revelations with us. Their generosity strengthens our courage to go on our own inner adventure. It is with gratitude that we enter into *She Reveals When It's Time*.

Letter to the Reader

Dear Precious One,

When our spiritual writing group was started, we had no idea how much our lives would be enriched, our hearts touched, our minds expanded and souls opened. That's what happens when a group of women meet, write and share their stories of a spiritual nature.

We reveal parts of ourselves that have been tucked away, sheltered, protected, unspoken, and parts that are sacred and precious. We reveal our beliefs, our joys, disappointments, our concerns, our relationships with ourselves, our families, our friends, and of course, with GOD. Through it all we laugh, we cry, we think, we remember and most importantly, we grow in consciousness. With this inner experience comes transformation.

In this book are a few of our stories that have been written with courage to share. When you read our stories, our hope is that something is sparked within you that opens your soul to discover your own voice and beliefs. In doing so, may you have your great reveal.

Blessings and love,
Martha

Dedication

To the women we were and the women we've become.

Special thanks to Bill Benitez of Positive Imaging, LLC for his publishing expertise, time, and generous support of this project.

Faith

Faith vs. Expectation
Martha Iglehart

The Dalai Lama once said, "Just as ripples spread out when a single pebble is dropped into water, the actions of individuals can have far reaching effects." I believe the same is true of our thoughts when we share them. They too can have far reaching effects.

Such was the case for this anecdote. Faith versus expectation began as a thought shared by one of our Spiritual Journey Writers in her essay one evening. We all pondered the statement as soon as she spoke it and at the end of the evening we decided to use it as a prompt for our next meeting. I was totally struck by the thought. It made my mind twirl and it hung with me for thoughtful consideration.

A few days later while sitting at work, a co-worker said to me, "I am losing my faith." Without giving her comment much thought I immediately said, "I heard a reading the other night that has me exploring faith."

I told her I was thinking of considering a new approach to faith. I shared with her how I arrived at the new consideration and said, "Instead of saying I have faith, say I expect."

From her came a big, "Ohhhhh! I don't think I agree with that. It doesn't feel right. My daddy would say that isn't right."

What ensued was very interesting. It sparked a conversation of considerable depth between a devout Catholic, a Charismatic preacher, a dedicated Jesus follower and several other Christians.

Our exchange of ideas and beliefs went back and forth and something just short of miraculous happened. We all agreed! We all agreed that if we approached life with greater expectancy, that GOD's goodness always prevails; we would stop living from a place of fear and live in a place of wonder and amazement. How magical would that be?

When comparing the two, faith (understood as a degree of belief) seems to be more passive than expectation. I know faith is the foundation of Christianity and all we need is a tiny bit to have a relationship with God. Perhaps it's the use of the word FAITH that makes it seem passive to me. When life seems to spin out of control and we can't make sense of it, we often hear, "Have faith." But if someone told me to EXPECT things to level off and to EXPECT everything will be okay, I'm more apt to single mindedly trust God with every ounce of my being. EXPECT seems to carry a greater charge of energy.

FAITH in God requires an inner knowing that is totally up to us to master. It's a power. It's an inner strength that only we can build, manifest and realize for ourselves.

I believe faith is the foundation of all that we are and desire, however I like the use of the word expect because it doesn't leave any wiggle room for doubts, or dual thoughts.

Now back to the ripples. When we finally finished our conversation that morning, the devout Catholic said with excitement and enthusiasm, "Now that was better than going to church!"

That one thought moved me to thinking when I first heard it. Days later it sparked a great conversation with several people coming at the concept with various ideas and beliefs. Just like actions of individuals can cause far reaching effects, so can a single thought. When a thought is shared, it can ripple out in all directions and have the power to create unity.

The Lion and The Lamb
(The King and the Sacrifice)
Sabrina Harris

I humbly and earnestly accept the crown of my divinity. I turn away from fear, worry, alienation, dependency and lies. I soar into the freedom of truth and join with my higher self as one. I stand tall allowing the crutches of ego to fall away from me. I let go of hatred, resentments, grudges and the desire to change the past. No longer will I suffer to make what was not so. I lay down my mediocre weapons of control, sarcasm, intimidation, condescension, and the limited weak and false sense of power that only brought forth bitter fruit. I drink from the fountain and eat the meat I know not of with abandon. I welcome the freedom to run at full speed treading the desire to be right, understood, heard, seen, and to impress beneath my feet. I no longer allow myself to be walled off and guarded. Good enough is no longer acceptable. I let go of the need to win and revel in being and becoming. I acknowledge my true loving nature with joy and excitement. I rest comfortably in the bright, clear day, openly and securely. I accept fully and wholly my crown and offer the sacrifice of my will with complete love and trust. I welcome knowing that the kingdom of heaven is within me and all is well. All is at peace.

Trust
Charlotte Brundrett

Sitting on my deck this morning, a sudden flurry of chattering and activity began just above my head in my big old hackberry. I always have two squirrels hanging around, but this morning there were four of them. They would race towards the end of the branches and then back to firmer limbs. Back and forth, chasing, and chattering.

I realized what they were working up to. They needed to be on the other side of the yard, onto the next set of trees, to get to wherever they were headed on their day's journey. Finally - one of them raced to the end of the limb - and jumped - and made it. In quick procession two others followed. The last little gal (or guy) stuttered about for a few seconds ... gave up and disappeared into the leaves. Needed more practice, I thought.

It made me think of the POWER of trust (my new favorite word). How do we trust? When do we trust? How much do we trust? And in what? Have you ever reached the end of the tree limb - abandoned all fear - and just leapt? Empowering, isn't it?

Trusting our trust. Just one of God's gifts.

When God Winks
Michelle Cheney

It was a few years ago, that I decided to venture to a new place in Europe. I opted to not go to countries where I had a small command of the language. I met a group of hikers, most Brits or Scots who liked the drink, but shared in a love of adventure and hiking the beautiful mountains where hungry locals had hidden their sons from Franco. I went to Spain.

The excursion took place in Andalusia, on the Southern tip of Spain, just a few miles from Gibraltar and a few more to Morocco. So yes, I journeyed to a place where the Moors had settled and lived and been destroyed by ambitious Christians.

The towns in this part of Spain have no streets. They are called "The White Villages" because the structures are marble white stucco, built centuries ago. The people of these towns, Torrox, Frigiliana, Ronda, continue to socialize by walking up and down alleys and walkways, decorated by tiny statues of Mary, fresh sills of flowers, open doorways, and intricate middle-eastern mosaics. Manchego cheese, blue hukka bars come cheap and found on alternate walkways.... There are few young people.

In the community of Torrox, where I lived for several days, I found a thriving pulse of life in the most different way. I'd rise early to wind my way to the town square, load up on bottled water and cheese and olives and cheap wine for hikes with new friends. There was the market, where I would giggle with vendors as I spoke Italian and they spoke Spanish, marveling at how well we could communicate in different languages. There was the young man Torrox locals looked after and fed and hushed, who yelled and suffered because of a fragile mind and there were many aged, sometimes deformed from less than adequate health care, who somehow hobbled up and down those white alleys in dark dresses and worn wedged shoes.

But it was the cats, yes, the cats, who held this prideful command of the white village- all well fed, and each appearing to be fully employed. I would pass them on my dizzying walks. The black and white one with the torn ear, the orange sleepy one, the Siamese mix with the arrogant attitude; they seemed to be as much of the community as the vendors or the café owners. I would say hello, nodding humbly to each perched on window ledges. Many of them pointed the way home.

Torrox is an hour from The Alhambra, that magical palace inhabited by Moore royalty, before being exiled by Ferdinand and Isabella, who eventually called it home. It's one of the wonders of the world, a marriage of math and art in the architecture. My plan was to rise very early, alone, and find a bus which would take me there.

That would be early, in the pitch black, in an ancient village, empty of life, hours before markets opened. I set my alarm clock for 5am. I barely slept.

To say I was a bit frightened is an understatement. So, as the door clicked shut behind me at my white cottage, I ventured off.
Very dark.
This alley, to that entrance?
Left?
Right?
The way wasn't familiar.
Would the moonlight help?
Which direction to the main highway?
I would be late. I was lost. I was very afraid.
I circled an ancient corner, no bigger than a tiny stall.

There they sat. About 15 of them. The blue moonlight made the vision clear, some with bodies low, elbows raised, others sitting upright, in sheer ecstasy, relishing the luxury of such wonderful company. No humans could provide better conversation.

Yes, the Siamese was there, the mangy fat orange one and the one with the tattered ear, along with at least a dozen feline locals. They resembled a band of old retired Italian men enjoying a coffee on a weekday morning, as they'd done for centuries. They all turned in unison and just looked at me, as if to say… "Yes,… do you need something?"

Dumbfounded, the only thing I could say, and I said it out loud, was "Excuse me, I didn't mean to interrupt. I'm so sorry." And I meant it. I had stepped into an ancient and sacred ritual of the cats of Torrox. It wasn't my place to explain or understand, and God winked at me and told me to laugh and that there were mysteries

and heart aches and fears that I would never understand
or believe or be able to explain with words…
And that it was time to find my bus.
And it was easy
And I did.

Nature

Love
Heather Bethea

I can move rocks,
And pave ways for new trails,
I can grow flowers,
And make dogs wag their happy tails.

If you watch me closely,
I have a rhythm and flow,
Though you may not understand it,
It's just for you to know.

To imagine life without me,
Well, there wouldn't be,
So consider me quite the necessity,
And relish in my gracious beauty.

Treat me with care,
And don't waste me,
I can give you years and years,
Of loving eternity.

I carry nutrients, renewal, vitality,
I feel energy, words and movement,
And bring it together in miraculous totality.

Sit back on a quiet day,
And enjoy my sweet stillness,
Or go ahead and jump in,
When the sun brings out your playfulness.

We can become one,
And you and I can get along,
I am a God given gift,
And I'm here for the long haul.

Love,
Water

My Sacred Place
Michelle Cheney

My Sacred Place. I've had a few in my life- places where solitude and dreams and fantasy have overcome the mundane pace of life.

The sacred places began when I was young, seven or eight - a beautiful meadow behind the sky blue trimmed house where I grew up.

I have always treasured a kind of romance in my loneliness, and sought isolation that sometimes isn't so undesirable. Raised in neighborhood packed with kids, all Mormon, except my brother and me, there was always a sense of being different, of having different desires or dreams. It was about that time, when I realized my differences, and I discovered a sacred place.

I was blessed to be born in the Wasatch Mountains, where creeks and streams brim in small canyons, and you don't have to journey far to find a soft patch of grass near the cool water in the Springtime. I remember the disappearing line of snow on the mountains, when the long winter was about to fade, and a yearning that I had to know more.

I have been drawn to my sacred places by my heart- a longing or a knowing that there was something beautiful and special if I just trusted…
And I remember how I came upon my first sacred place, the meadow, just five minutes from my home…

The meadow must have been a yard or garden to a farm that had been abandoned decades ago. Tulips popped in the spring, Lilacs blossomed in May, Summer offered plumbs. A soft green grass was surrounded by trees, isolated. It was there that I fantasized about solving mysteries, finding treasures from early pioneers, imagined being a famous dancer, or finding some clue to a question that wasn't even asked. I believed it was the secret place, the sacred place, that was familiar to no one.

It's gone now. A large house has devoured its sweetness, but the magic stays.

In Crested Butte, Colorado, there is a long thin road that takes you to a small garden of stones. There is something other worldly and ancient about it. As an adult I would wander with girlfriends in the summer, toting baseball hats, sunscreen, nuts and wine, looking for adventure, looking for beauty.

So what was it to drive me down that thin trail, with so few markings? And why was it so easy to find a small sanctuary with a cross and benches at the base of a creek on that trail? And was that really an owl sitting in the tree above me when I said my prayers in that sacred place? Was that yet another sacred place that I can call upon when I need the nurturing, one that I discovered with my heart and not a map?

The final sacred place sits in my nightstand, next to me when I sleep; my grandmother's rosary, five angels representing Trust, Faith, Joy, Courage and Love to touch when I am hurting, a journal to release my dreams and fears and five books with spiritual thoughts. Each morning, I touch them, I read them, I feel the same connection on my heart that I feel in the mountains or near a stream. Each day, I can touch my sacred place.

Seasons of Change
Carol Moncada

The swaying of the bougainvillea, the rustling of leaves, the tinkling sound of wind chimes announce the arrival of a cool front this morning. Just like that another season has arrived. I have been waiting for it, wondering where it was. It has subtly been moving into a new season all along. You can see it in the accelerated activity of the squirrels as they hunt, gather, dig and bury provisions for the coming winter; the grape vine as it loses more of its leaves, the summer flowers dying back to rest until rebirth in the Spring. Yes, the seasons are in constant motion, coming around again and again, renewed and refreshed. It is the subtleties that we fail to take note of, only acknowledging the larger effects such as the drastic drop in temperatures.

Life is full of seasons of change, and like the seasons, we often miss the subtleties, the continual motion of a greater life within us, waiting to be acknowledged, to be released, to be expressed. Life is full of opportunities to change, to let go of the past versions of ourselves and to create a bigger vision. We hesitate, we fear, we talk ourselves down, or dismiss our dreams. We hold onto an old idea of our selves that wasn't ours to begin with. Did you hear me? We hold onto an idea of who we are that wasn't ours to begin with.

We often think of seasons of change within our own lives as growing older and of drastic changes that have come from momentous life events. Yes, those do create changes that we cannot ignore. But what if we looked at seasons of change differently? As the leaves turn color and drop from the trees, perhaps that could be our season of looking at the old stories of ourselves and dropping them. Perhaps it can be our season of looking at how we have judged others, and let those judgements flitter away. As we scrape and carve our pumpkins, let us scrape clean our souls too. Let us become empty vessels for the quiet of the Winter season to fill us, so that rebirth can happen in the Spring and multiply in the season of our Summer. The Seasons are in constant motion, life is in constant living. We, the created, are constantly creating our own seasons of change, if we but take note, and guide it through to its rightful expression. Remembering that the Spring does not hang on to the dead leaves of the Fall, but allows the metamorphosis that has been going on in the inner chambers of its Winter season to come forth. Being present to and flowing with our own seasons of change provides us with the opportunity to bring forth a greater expression of ourselves, our own vision of our self that is authentic, that is true.

The sun sits lower in the sky, the leaves fall softly on the ground, the rose has lost its last petal of its summer season. And I take note, as I too gently let go the petals of my past seasons and open up to the new seasons of change within me.

A Sacred Space
Janice Goodsell

One of my sacred spaces is Rocky Mountain National Park in Colorado. I don't remember exactly how long we were living in Denver before we visited Rocky, but I fell in love with it from the beginning. Oh those beautiful mountains, and the rushing waters, and the smell of Ponderosa Pine. How the air is cool and the sun is your summertime friend and you don't want to leave it. How at every bend in the road or trail, one might see a majestic animal or a waterfall, or a mountain scene that takes your breath away. And Trail Ridge Road - a natural wonder in a category all by itself. Winding higher and higher, walking the alpine trail slowly, huffing and puffing due to the thin air; finding a snowbank next to the road in July, filling the playing people with pure joy and wonder; still visible Native American trails from summer visits in centuries past; it is one "Sound of Music" mountain scene after another.

When you live in Colorado, you have a **lot** of out-of-state visitors, and every time we had visitors we took them here. My step-daughter coming for a long summer visit: take her camping at Rocky. Dave's sister with four children under the age of 12 staying for two weeks: take them camping at Rocky. Hoping to convince my grown daughters to move here: take them camping at Rocky. Trying to make a big impression on Texan friends: take them camping at Rocky. It was a steady item on my entertainment list.

And my husband Dave and I often headed here just for ourselves. This was where I heard my first elk bugle in the middle of a September night, saw my first moose grazing in a meadow, where Dave saw his first shooting star in the cold, crisp air of winter. Here is where I learned forbearance: to leave the wildflower unpicked, to leave that fascinating rock in its place. We camped surrounded by snowbanks, overshadowed by Fall Aspen colors, and enveloped by the cool summer nights. Now when I go on my August visits, I take my grandchildren and pass down my love of this sacred place.

This year I will not be camping at Rocky. Eight hours after summer registration opened, there were no spots available for more than one day at a time. So many more people from all over the world are loving Rocky Mountain National Park too! We will be camping in other Colorado mountains, so perhaps I shall begin an adventure with a new sacred space. But, Rocky Mountain National Park will always come first, for in my heart "all the trails are downhill".

Humanity

Human Rights
Carol Moncada

Those two words, Human rights, can conjure up all sorts of mental images and meanings. In a time of great divisiveness in our nation, many fear the loss of some of their human rights. So, what are "human rights"? One way to define it is: rights (as freedom from unlawful imprisonment, torture, and execution) regarded as belonging fundamentally to all people. We think of our civil liberties, of our constitutional rights, of our inalienable rights. This is important, and we must stand up for all peoples' rights. We must stand up to constitutions and laws that restrict, persecute and limit a person's rights in any way.

There is another way in which to look at Human Rights. It is through the perspective of our Spiritual nature. We are expressions of our Creator who has given us inalienable rights in our human form. Foremost, is our own will. We get to choose how we show up in this dimension. We get to choose to claim our rights, our powers, as children of God, or not. Mostly, we do not.

We have the right to happiness and joy. Yet we choose sadness, anger and despair. We have the right to an abundant life, and yet we choose to believe that there is only lack. We have the right to wholeness and to heal ourselves, but choose to believe in suffering, illness and physical death.

We make a mess of our lives, of our nation, of our earth, because we do not comprehend our human rights. We do not follow Law. Spiritual Law. We imprison ourselves with false belief systems that say we cannot be, do or have that which is rightfully ours. That which we rightfully are.

When we embrace both our humanity and our divinity, live from that, then we will know freedom. But our responsibility doesn't end there, we must also ensure that all our brothers and sisters know their human rights. That they too can live fully in their humanity and their divinity and know true freedom.

We have a choice. When we will choose freedom? When will we choose to stand up and stand in our human rights as Spiritual beings? How long can the world continue to wait?

Loss

Dear Anonymous
(Shut the door)
Sabrina Harris

I have not been to our twelve-step meeting in a couple of weeks. I have been leaning into my other program working the steps and trying to save my life. I was finishing up chairing the meeting in my other program, rushing to gather things together, grab a couple of hugs, and get the heck out of there, because I had work in the morning. During my rush, a member who also shares our program came over to me. I was glad to see her and pulled her close to sit next to me. I had found papers in the meeting materials with her name on them and, as a dutiful chair, handed the papers to her to see if they were hers. I felt relief when she recognized them and claimed them. My duty was done. She was quiet for a moment and then said, "I have sad news". I then heard her say your name and the words committed suicide. I was trying to be sure I heard her correctly. Her words were swimming around inside me. I was shocked and heard myself say, "I'm stunned." I did not want to believe what she said but her face was serious, and her green eyes were locked on mine. She then gave me the month and the date you died. In that moment I was shaken and disturbed. I felt like I was standing on a lake of ice that had begun to crack between my feet and I didn't know which way to jump for safety, hoping instinct would take over. I felt weak and helpless. You gave no warning and managed to slip away from me just beyond my reach. I heard our friend say, "It just shows you relationships can kill you too." I nodded in agreement as I was searching to find an inner grounding or center, and gain repossession of myself.

I remembered why I had the meeting materials in my hands and put them where they belonged. I think a couple of folks hugged me as I made my way to my car then, managed to drive home. I probably had on music, but I was driving on autopilot too aware of my breath. There was a burning feeling in my chest where my heart was moving things around for your permanent place to live with the month, date and year of your death. They reside with the few memories I have of you and the wish that we had touched, hugged or that I had kissed your forehead. That is an annoying thing I do to people who are shorter than I am. Rarely do I see people hug in our meetings. I suppose I was preoccupied with whether I belonged there.

You had been on my mind recently before I got the news. I wondered where you were and why you hadn't been coming to meetings. This often happens to me where I discover someone dancing among my thoughts and then suddenly, they call me or show up somehow. It happens far too often to consider random or coincidence. It is one reason I believe there is more than the earth life we know. I don't exactly have my arms around it, but I know there is more. I have a lot of questions. When you shut the door did you meet the angels? Are you free now, darling? Are you conscious of the heavy sadness and loss I feel for you? Can you feel me holding you in my heart, in that place? Can you taste the tears that well up in my eyes love? How long will my heart ache and burn? Ok, I admit my ego is in this. What did

I miss? What could I have done? I don't think you really gave me a chance, dear. I want to be angry with you, but I feel so much hurt from the loss and for the pain you must have endured to bring you to take your life. Ok, ok, I admit some mild frustration with you, but mostly hurt and bewilderment. I *can* tell you I'm getting help. I've reached out for support and gotten it as the programs teach us to do. I miss seeing you and what we didn't get to have. You shut the door and made an opening in my heart. God bless you always, sweetheart, and goodbye to what we may have thought we knew.

Angels

Angel Among Us, Like a Kiss on the Forehead
Carol Moncada

I spread my arms wide and I am running. No, I am flying and she stands behind me laughing with me as I circle back to be embraced with a kiss on the forehead.

I feel beautiful as I twirl in my new dress and yet too scared to step onto the stage. She squeezes my hand, and with a kiss on the forehead, lets go. I feel her love flow through me into the keys beneath my fingers and I forget everything but the music.

It's blue velvet, soft against my skin. A suit she made from her own pattern. Because she remembers her first dance. She remembers wanting to feel magical. With a kiss on the forehead, in my new blue velvet suit, I am magical.

I squeeze her hand too tightly. She doesn't complain. She doesn't flinch. She patiently waits, and with a kiss on the forehead, encircles her new granddaughter and me with her love.

She braids his hair and with a kiss on the forehead, hands me my bouquet. My dress is gold, but she sparkles with love. She gains another son today.

I hear a soft flutter, feel the gentlest of touches, a kiss on the forehead. I am engulfed in love. And I know before I open my eyes, she has gone.

The thorn brings bright red blood as I tend the rose bush. She brought it from Kansas all those many years ago. I feel her love in that moment, an angel among us, like a kiss on the forehead.

One laughs like her, another has her humor. One cooks like her, and yet another one is quietly confident like her. Her love is reflected through these girls, our daughters, angels among us, like a kiss on the forehead.

I spread my arms wide and I am running. No, I am flying and she stands beside me, I feel her love enfold me, an angel among us, like a kiss on the forehead.

ANGELS
Sara Stewart

Do you believe in Angels? Where are they? What do they look like?

Do they eat, sleep, sing, dance, laugh, or cry like you and me???

Yes, I believe in Angels. I believe they come in all shapes and sizes; different colors and even different species.

They protect us from harm and surround us with love or remind us we are loved, needed and wanted often when we need it the most.

I believe Angels come in the form of....

A touch from a child, a friend or a lover

A smile, a glance, a wink or a nod

A lick or the wag of a tail

A scent that triggers a feeling or a memory of days gone by

Butterflies, birds, flowers, music...

I feel I know for sure there are Angels among us; watching over us; protecting us from harm in car accidents or not having a car accident

Letting me "know" my father was going to be gone soon and to enjoy the time we had left

Washing my mother's feet during her bath just minutes before she died

Beautiful sunrises and sunsets

Playing as a child and feeling that all is right with the world

Talking to animals with animal sounds, looks and touches

And yes, sometimes I see their images in hearts, in wings, in clouds, on walls… in so many different ways

Stop… look… listen on the outside and within

Sometimes in a rolling thunder, sometimes in a whisper but

Always, in all ways they are around

Never fear… Your Angels Are Here

Angels
Sabrina Harris

I want to believe they're real and on the side of good. I have read about them, spoken to them, asked favors of them, and believed at times they were near. I've wanted to be an angel and live in the invisible, where it's obvious that all things are possible, and truth is truth. I've wanted angel wings to fly and soar higher and higher, then gracefully glide to the earth ever so gently. They would be huge, beautiful wings, soft and light, yet luscious. I want to believe I'm watched over and loved, even adored. I want to feel legitimized in helping and doing good. I want to answer a child's prayer. I want to touch an adult who has given up and help them find the reason to go on. I want to pour out oceans of love and watch life drink it in. I want to be free and know what it's like to relax and stretch out on a cloud absorbing the sounds of the universe. I want to communicate with the animals and know them in a way that I can feel my oneness with them. Angels, I want to be an angel. Where do I register?

Are WE Angels
Martha Iglehart

Are WE angels? None of us can probably know for certain, but this is what I believe.

Light, calmness, peaceful silence, order amid chaos and unsolicited help in the middle of trouble. These are a few signs that let us know they are all around us. Who? OUR angels.

They're in our midst, in our seen and unseen worlds, showing up as little children, friends, distant relatives, strangers and even our animals. Angels are present at just the right time, in inexplicable ways, to bring us relief from disasters and discomfort and to celebrate us in our moments of triumph. They are with us whether it's on a physical, emotional, psychological or spiritual level.

Angels show up with the perfect message, or an outstanding act of kindness. They help us awaken to an understanding of things ordinarily too complex to comprehend in order for us to grow and advance on our spiritual path. They help us realize our faith power.

Thus, I believe angels are moved by the creator of this great universe to act on our behalf. They show up at the right place and time to touch us on a deep level because being touched on the surface is too easily overlooked. Angels operate in ways to affirm they are real and they operate in ways to remind us that the unseen world is a reality too.

So are WE angels? I believe that if at anytime we act from a higher state of consciousness to share kind words, offer a helping hand, or lovingly carry out a thoughtful deed to help another avoid harm or bondage, WE too will be recognized as angels.

Intuition

My Inner Voice
Sara Stewart

Like most of us my inner voice likes to talk a lot. She has definite opinions; she always thinks she is right; that she knows best and if everyone would only listen to her the world would be a much better place. There would be abundant, abiding love.

Sometimes my inner voice—more than I would like— fusses at me and tells me everything that is wrong with me; how hopeless I am; that I will never be happy; That I will never have the good things that I want like a home, children, enough money to share and money to spare, a man who loves me just as I am…

And then thank goodness there is the deeper, deepest inner voice that tells me the Truth of who I am

That I am a child of God; I am loved by God

That God has a plan or me and for my life

That he doesn't give more than I can handle- especially when I remember to ask for his help

I am whole, healed, healthy, loved, prosperous and intelligent

I have all the faith I need and

I lead others by example… I shine my Light for all to see so

WE CAN BECOME ALL GOD WANTS US TO BE!

My Inner Voice
Martha Iglehart

There are so many voices in my inner galaxy. "Turn some of these lights off. Electricity is not free!" I hear that voice often when I walk around my house and notice I have lights on that aren't needed. It's my mother's voice. I keep waiting for it to fade since she passed away over five years ago, but her voice has become a permanent resident inside my heart.

"Go ahead. You can do it. You've got it in you to do it." That was also my mother. That voice is less scolding, and comes more in the tone of encouragement and inspiration.

Then there is my other voice that speaks constant thoughts. Thoughts of decisions, doubts, far-fetched ideas, fears, and answers to fill in the blanks of stories left incomplete or untold. I call it my monkey-mind voice. That voice gets a lot of game time. They say we can have over 60,000 thoughts a day. As tiresome as that may sound, the voice of my monkey-mind seldom tires out. It's speaking right now. It's saying to me, "*As you are sharing this story, do you think people will think you're crazy, or do you think they will identify with what you are saying?*" Rarely, during conscious moments, does it shut down.

Yet, separate from those voices is another voice. It's a quiet voice audible only to me. When it speaks, it's more like an inner discovery that shows me solutions and fills every ounce of my being with a knowing and an assurance of its message. It vibrates and resonates at such a high frequency that I know this isn't my monkey-mind having a thought. This is something coming through me from beyond my inner galaxy. This voice is my higher self, my Master, MY GOD speaking to me. This voice is never critical. It speaks in silence and images. Yes images. I can see what it is saying to me with deep understanding. This voice that is silent moves me to feel its message and takes me above and beyond my ego. There's no room for questions…only clarity. There's nothing haunting about this voice. It's not frightening at all. I can't control it.

Unlike the voice that comes with my monkey-mind, I can visualize what my silent voice tells me. The monkey-mind voice is predictable. The silent voice is not. And it's so powerful it can shut down the voice of the monkey-mind. It takes center stage and all I can do is surrender to it calmly and eagerly and honor its message. It's my silent voice.

Silent voice so loud & clear,

Whispers wisdom my heart holds dear.

Never to scare me or cause me fear

But to remind me MY GOD is near.

It's creative, it's wise, it's loving, it's kind,

Always sounding off in the nick of time.

It's my friend, my partner, my confidant, my mate.

There to shift my consciousness from complex states,

Like moments of fear, doubt, confusion, despair.

I never have to seek it, I just listen….it's there.

Silent voice so loud & clear,

I'm so grateful you're always near.

Grace Reflection

A Letter From God
Amanda Kuda

I'm sitting in a luxe covered cabana on the beach. I've lucked into the spot on the account that the beach is desolate this time of year. I've just finished a fancy breakfast served with too many cups of coffee. I ate overlooking the ocean as I finished the last few pages of the cute romantic novel I'd brought along. I agreed to another cup of coffee while holding back tears behind my sunglasses as I reached the emotional ending of my book.

I found my way, then, to the beachside cabanas, filled with a whimsy I often get after reading a good book. I sit cross-legged on my beach bed, staring into the water and breathing slowly. The pages of my journal are filled with scribbles of gratitudes and intentions and letters to God. I write intermittently all morning, stopping often to stare into the waves. Sometimes to cry tears of overwhelm and excitement and joy.

I'm so grateful to have this time alone. I have no schedule. No agenda. No one else to please. I have only myself. I sit for hours, letting the sun hit my face.

I ask for answers, for certainty, for clarity, for grace. This is what I know: I have work to do; work that is far greater than what I can accomplish at a simple 9-5 job. I am to be a guide for others. I write the words in my journal mechanically and fill several additional pages.

My writing changes tone and voice until finally, I have written this:

Stop weighing yourself down with the secret fear that you are not supported. You are. You are so splendidly and perfectly supported, but only - you have weighed yourself down with an undue and false burden of lack. You have taken on the story that you are not enough as you are. That your dreams are too big. That "it" can happen, just not for you.

You have shouldered the weight of this fear for too long. Step into your power. Step into your light. Let go of your fear that it might shine with too much intensity. Release the tiny voice that whispers the lie that you are not supported because, darling, YOU ARE.

There is a Universe ready and waiting to conspire on your behalf. There is a plan which will unfold so perfectly you will hardly believe it. It is there if you will only release your need to be in control. Listen to me when I say that no matter how big your dreams, they are still small-minded in comparison to what is in store for you if you allow yourself to believe this light and beautiful truth: you are supported FULLY, wildly & unimaginably supported.

I re-read the passage from my journal again and wonder for a moment if I might have copied it from somewhere. But then, from where? It had been written while I sat on a deserted beach, completely disconnected. It surely came from me...or rather, through me. But I read it again, just to be sure. My journal is filled with more pages of scribbles from my time on the beach. Most are notes to God. This one stands out because it is a note from God to me.

Shut The Door
Heather Bethea

I walk into this house; a beautifully built home which smells of old wood and aromas from the kitchen. The door is open and welcoming. You can't help but to want to walk in.

There are several bedrooms filled with a variety of decorations, liveliness, hanging posters, flowers, memories and remnants from many lives of the past.

The living room is soft and warm and has a dim glow that welcomes anyone's presence. Old antique furniture fills the room with robustness, yet gentleness. You can gently hear the wind chimes that hang themselves outside the living room window.

It's a strong house and it has had its share of many memories. People have come through, visited, stayed for awhile, and some have left without truly understanding its value. It has endured change, lots and lots of change. There have been thunderstorms, neglect, its friends around being torn down, yet, throughout all of it, the house stood strong and always opened its door to anyone desiring to come in.

Every morning as the sun rises upon its front door and shines so eloquently through the windows, the house welcomes the new day. It finds itself excited for what the day may hold.

Who will come visit, what will be brewing in the kitchen, what conversations will be heard throughout the home - will there be tears, joy, laughter, worry? The house opens itself to it all; as a beacon of support and comfort.

Approaching sunset, the calmness sets in after a long, and busy day. The sun falls steadily to its end for the day and the house knows what this means.

Night is coming upon it, and soon the quiet will be heard. As the house gets ready for sweet slumber, it tidies up from the day, turns the AC down just a little, lights a candle and rests.

The mere sweetness of home sets in and the house releases a sigh of relief for another blessed day...and shuts the door. But only until tomorrow.

Reflections at the Clothesline
Janice Goodsell

Today I hang my laundry outside to dry. This is something I love to do and actually do, whenever weather and time allow. As I calculate how much line space to give each item and how many pins I can grasp in one hand, I see a Fritillary butterfly hovering around my passionflower vine that smells so wonderfully fresh and sweet. The sun is warm and I feel a small trickle of sweat trailing down my back. Suddenly a southeasterly breeze comes up, sending sheets and towels to billow in the breeze. I am taken back, back, back in time to another clothesline with blowing sheets and towels from a flower-scented wind on another hot summer's day, in my childhood country home in Alabama.

My mother has filled the long, long clotheslines as she always does on laundry-day, for clothes dryers are an unknown luxury. The sheets and towels pop and twist in the wind, and give off a clean smell that augments the smell of the vetch and sarissa fields that surround our lawn. My sisters and I spread a quilt in the protected, cool shade beneath our huge maple tree. We carefully place our glasses of Kool aid out of the way of our bare feet. Then the box of paper dolls comes out and the sorting of folders, paper dolls and their paper clothes begins. The folders are rooms of our houses, and the paper clothes are stacked in each paper doll's bedroom.

Now it's time to make our families. Fathers are selected from paper dolls of George Montgomery, Pat Boone, Roy Rogers or Desi Arnaz. Mothers are selected from Dinah Shore, Elizabeth Taylor, Gale Storm, June Allyson, Lucille Ball, Dale Evans, Jane Powell or Doris Day. Annette Funicello and the Lennon sisters are our teenagers; generic boys, girls and babies of no particular fame are the children, except for Little Ricky and Dusty. There are even a few family pets.

We give each family member our favorite names that usually change with each play time, although there is a pet dog that we always name "Dopey". Our paper dolls go to school, play with each other, go to parties, have fights and then make up. Sometimes they pile into a folder car and go to the movies or on a vacation. We have no personal experience of anyone taking a vacation except for Aunt Elene, so we draw on our imagination, or go by what we've seen on television. My older sister supplies us with names of destinations: New York, Los Angeles, San Francisco, and Chicago, cities that seem so exotic. Actually any city sounds exotic, since we have never been to a town larger than Huntsville, which at the time has a population of about 40,000.

But our paper dolls know these cities, and they go to museums, libraries, parks; big fancy department stores with revolving doors and escalators. They go to the beach and rent cabins in the mountains. Many happy pleasant hours we spend this way. Funny how those memories are brought back to life, by the sight and smell of clothes drying in the sun and breeze on another hot summer day. My heart feels so light. All's right with the world; I love the whole world. All my life I hope to be hanging out clothes!

Belief

Letter to a Woman on the Verge
Amanda Kuda

You, dear woman, are brilliant, brave, resilient and capable.
You are loved.
You are enough.
You are on the verge of something magnificent.
Lean into your brilliance, even when it is hard.
Especially when it is hard.

Because, the truth is, it will often be hard.
It will seem like you are going through something more intense than those around you.
You are.
But, it is because you have a dream on your heart that most people don't dare to dream.
You have heard the rumbling of your soul.
And, once you hear it's subtle call, you cannot un-hear it.

Try as you might, you will **never** un-hear it.
It's frightening, isn't it? The notion that you are meant for something tremendous and great?
The thought that you are capable of so much more than you have allowed yourself to achieve; I know it's intimidating.

My dear, do not let yourself be frightened.
You would not be given the thought of a dream if it were not yours to have.
Whatever it is that you desire, it was meant for you.

All that you need - the people, the money, the resources, the knowledge - they will all appear in divine timing if only you are willing to trust in your ability to be great.
I know it all seems quite impossible,
That the pieces would just fall into place with your little bit of willingness.
They will.

But, let me warn you, do not place many expectations on what your path will look like.
Release control of how you might get there because the path will not look as you expect.
Despite how hard you might try,
You are not in charge of the path, you are only in charge of walking.
The path will be laid before you,
Perfectly designed and orchestrated in a way that you could never imagine.
It is only your job to walk.
To put one foot in front of the other.
Even when it feels like you are trudging through quicksand.
Continue to walk.

Do not let your fears,
Or your current perception of your capabilities,
Or your resources,
Or the thoughts of others
Keep you small.

Rather, hold that thought, that dream.
Hold on tightly to it in your mind.

Feel the deep sense of knowing that it is absolutely intended to be yours.
And, with that, the only thing that can truly hold you back from having it is you.

Do not, for one more second,
Let your own fears and insecurities hold you back.
Do not, for another instant
Compare your journey to the journey of others.
Do not give one ounce of credibility to the notion that you are not enough.
You are.
You are more than enough, and that thought can be scary.
But, rest assured,
You beautiful,
Strong,
Capable,
Resilient,
Wonderful woman...you are absolutely enough and you are on the verge of something truly magnificent.

My Sacred Place
Sara Stewart

My mind first thinks of a physical location where I feel safe, secure and at ease to be myself. So many places I think of like Sedona, Santa Fe, and places I have only read about but something about them resonates with me-- my wish for adventure; exploring different cultures; learning about what life is like for others in different areas of the world.

And then I think any place can be a Sacred Place. It is only dependent on my state of mind. What about that Sacred Place inside of me? Where is it? What does it want to tell me? What does it want from me?

I feel my Sacred Place physically in my heart and in my hands. Connecting with my Sacred Place it tells me:

I am loved; I am worthy; I am enough. I have unlimited Good. I have unlimited talent, unlimited love, peace and joy to share and all the room I need to accept these things; all the strength to accept these things. It tells me to give myself a break. Lighten up on myself, lighten up on others. It needs me to connect with it every day even if it is just a moment or two.

The World is a Sacred Place. I am a part of that World, I am a part of this World and I am Sacred to myself and others and to God and Jesus.

Stay true to the Spirit within you. I am there to guide you on a beautiful journey.

My home is Sacred

My job is Sacred

My Life is Sacred

My health is Sacred

My family is Sacred

My joy is Sacred

My trust is Sacred

My heart is Sacred

My friends are Sacred

My pets are Sacred

My car is Sacred

My physical, mental and emotional health are Sacred.

Treat it all with respect. Give yourself as much respect as you give others.

You are worth it. You are my Sacred Place.

A Sacred place is a state of mind not dependent upon my mind but upon the state of my Heart.

Myths
Ann-Marie Fontenot

She was baptized Estelle Marie Fontenot, the second child of Gilbert Fontenot, cotton sharecropper in South Louisiana. Acquaintances knew her as Estelle or Mary. I knew her as "Mama."

As a child, I realized that my mother was devoted to the Blessed Virgin Mary. Mama knew all about the Virgin Mary's life and prayed to her daily. Mama even purchased a concrete statue of the Blessed Mother from the Rosary House in New Iberia and had the statue placed in the front yard of our house. She then adorned the statue with a rose-covered trellis erected over it.

Mama informed me that the Blessed Mother's favorite color was blue. I knew that this was true, because Mama kept a five-inch tall plastic statue of the Blessed Virgin Mary on her dressing table in her bathroom (next to a plastic crucifix of Jesus). The statue of the Blessed Mother was blue: her hair, face, eyes, hands, and feet, as well as her headpiece and long dress, were all blue. As a child, I took my mother's word for it: Mary's favorite color was blue. And so was my mother's favorite color: blue.

As I grew older, more educated, and more savvy in my thinking, I began to question the figure that Mama painted of the Blessed Mother. No human could be as good as my mother described Mary to be. I eventually considered the mother of Jesus and all the stories that were attributed to her to be myths. My mother was clearly misinformed about this character and, to my amusement, unwittingly worshiped a pagan goddess. How horrified Mama would have been if I had informed her of the truth!

Fortunately, I never attempted to correct Mama's faulty thinking. Growing up in my family, with its particular issues, captured most of my attention. Mama built and operated her own business, while struggling with alcoholic problems in her spouse during an era when there was little knowledge and much misunderstanding about the disease. At the same time, she managed to raise a family of seven children. Mama was immersed in a man's world in the Deep South in the 1940's and 1950's. Despite criticisms leveled at her efforts by local male entrepreneurs, my mother was successful in her endeavors: her business became the most lucrative one in the town; and my siblings and I were all well-provided for.

Only in the last year did I discover that Mama was not named "Mary." She was named "Marie." Even my siblings – when I asked them, "What was Mama's name?" Answered "Mary Estelle." I've had them look at their birth certificates to read their mother's name. Each has been surprised to read that her legal name was Estelle Marie. However, Mama told everyone that her name was "Mary." Maybe she was embarrassed of her French Acadian heritage; but, I believe that she wanted to identify with the mother of Jesus, thereby calling herself "Mary."

Perhaps the myth of the Blessed Mother was God's gift of inspiration to Mama. Jesus's mother is a role model for a woman to emulate. The concept of the Blessed Mother provided my mother what she needed to survive and support her family of seven in an environment that was less than accepting and sometimes hostile to our family's well-being. Despite my personal opinion about the figure of the Blessed Virgin, Mama's strong belief in the Mother of Jesus remained intact throughout Mama's life, sustaining and lifting her above her human nature. My mother's attachment to this holy woman connected Mama to the Divine, provided a model of acceptance of God's will for her, and offered on-going hope and strength to carry out God's will "day after day." Today, the statue of the Blessed Mother is gone from the front yard of our house. Mama is gone, too. But, I have no doubt that she is seated on a throne at the right hand of the Blessed Virgin Mary . . . Mama's divine model and forever companion.

Standing in the Truth
Frances Beckley

While I was living in Majuro, Marshall Islands in the 90's, I led a bible-based discussion group once a week. I invited everyone I knew, including strangers that had just arrived for a conference or government work. All religions were represented except Mormons who would not come. I used books I had received from friends at a Methodist church in Upstate New York. We read the Old Testament and New Testament. I introduced them to meditation and eventually meditation became part of our meeting.

Our discussions were sometimes loud and angry, as there were so many different thoughts and beliefs. I stood fast saying, "My God doesn't say that," and if asked, I'd explained.

Joining our group was a missionary. Betty served in Africa…very set in her beliefs and doctrine. After about two-years she turned to me and said, "Teach me about your God within." I explained everything I knew… all the ways God talked to me…and how I see God everywhere. When Betty left to return to her mission in Africa, she wrote and said, "I will teach others about God within and have them see and feel the Christ." We stayed in touch until she died three-years later.

Many people in our group only stayed a few months. I received many thank you notes for the information they received. I gained insight into their beliefs. One couple from Tonga wrote, "You didn't try to change our religion. You let us learn, and we found God within while still allowing us to grow stronger in our faith. Thank you. We are sharing the Christ/God within, with others."

Recently I was at Jim's Restaurant (I go there often) and my waitress asked what I was doing. I told her I'd written the 23rd Psalms into my own words and she said, "Read it to me."

The Lord God is my companion and I need nothing because you are always with me.

You make a place for me to lie down in safety and comfort.

You lead me by restful waters that refresh my soul.

You guide me on the right path that makes me secure.

Even when I falter you comfort me, reassure me and guide me.

You are always with me, anointing me with wisdom, knowledge, goodness and love, and I will be with you all the days of my life.

When I finished and looked up, tears were flowing. "Do you really believe God is with you?" she asked.

"Yes," I replied.

"Did you think God would be with me?"

I said, "He is always with you, even now."

"Please write this for me."

I gave her a copy. As I left Jim's, a man who I had never seen followed me to my car and said, "I see your light…it is shining very bright. I have been watching you for two days and your light surrounds you and others."

"Thank you," I said, and I never saw the man again. The next day the waitress said she repeated the Psalms many times until she knew God was there. She has shared it with others. An elderly man said he wants it to be read at his grave and wanted my permission. He wrote it in his will and has shared it with others also.

When asked what I believe, I share what I know and feel in my sacred place within.

I close my writing with my version of the Lord's Prayer.

Our God who is everywhere.

Praise your Holy Name.

Guide us as we enter the kingdom within receiving knowledge and understanding.

Let your desire for us become our desire to glorify your Holy Name.

Thank you for our daily gifts.

Forgive us our errors as we forgive others.

Lead us on a righteousness path so we may resist temptation.

We praise you forever and ever.

AMEN.

Love

If I Could...
Ann-Marie Fontenot

...Pack my backpack with Life's delights and fly to a distant land, I would arrive with a smile on my heart and open arms to embrace my loved ones, who, until now, do not know me.

I would step ashore into a sea of faces peering intently into my eyes, their own eyes searching for signs of acceptance and friendliness. The children, clinging to their mothers' legs or staring at me unabashedly from the safety of their mothers' arms, are the first to return my smile - if they have not already cried out in fright at the sight of my silver hair!

My new acquaintances reach forward to relieve me of my backpack. We lay it on the ground. A young boy, prodded by his father, pushes through the crowd to offer me a cup of water. I squat down to open my bag and hand him a harmonica, small enough to fit in his pocket. Grinning, he returns to his father's side and the crowd presses in to see what other treasures emerge from my backpack. Each person receives a gift. Balloons, balls, playing cards, and pocket-sized cars for the boys; barrettes, hair ribbons, necklaces, and bracelets for the girls; socks, slippers, hats, and scarves for the adults. I hear squeals of delight and feel the warmth of smiles surrounding me. Pleasure abounds!

A bonfire is started. Music, soft and rhythmic, ripples through the evening air. The women begin to dance...

slowly… with grace. The festivities wear on with food, laughter, and babies nodding off to sleep at their mothers' breasts.

Picking up my empty bag, I stand up, admiring my beautiful family. Our connection is complete: our hearts are united and my soul's thirst is satisfied.

The crowd walks with me to the shore. We lovingly touch hands and exchange smiles before I nod and disappear into the darkness. I am fulfilled.

Love
Janice Goodsell

What can I write about love? Love is a feeling, a feeling that has been written about so often by so many people that anything I say will be redundant. Hasn't it all already been said?

My spontaneous thought is that I don't really know what love is, but that cannot be true. I have to have some kind of idea after living this many years. I'm trying to figure it out. Yes, I'm still breathing and still trying to figure it out.

Is love a verb or a noun? At one time I thought of love as duty, fondness or a desire for a relationship – familiarity or hormones – but now I'm thinking it's something more like acceptance. Not worrying about a person having this characteristic or that asset; not caring who loves who first or even if they love me back.

David Hawkins defines love as "the energy that radiates when the blocks to it have been surrendered." This resonates with me. This says love is just there, it's a part of me. It is energy, always there, and I would love unconditionally if I didn't have these false safeguards I've erected to hold myself apart. I created the blocks and I can surrender them when I face my fears and choose to let them go.

As I get older, I get smarter. I am a more loving person and I experience more joy. I try to recognize when I'm not being loving, and I do recognize I probably am unconscious to much of it. Although my first reaction can be defensive when another points it out to me, I am grateful to them. I know they have done me a favor.

I really like what The Daily Word said today: "I look at the world through the eyes of love and focus on the good in each person and situation I encounter. If I cannot find the good, I lean on my faith in God and trust that the omnipresent power of love is always present". There is so much going on right now in our government that I want to change. My challenge is to have the incentive to work for change as I am being a loving person. There are so many moments when I cannot seem to find the good, when my emotions and fears leap to life. Remember, Janice, love is always present and available. I will find the balance: to love myself as God loves me.

"Love, love, love, love. The gospel in one word is love." This is the song I sing to my granddaughter. May my life show her in a small way what love is.

She Is You
Heather Bethea

I see this woman. She is vibrant, she is happy, she is love.

Her physical body is graceful, healthy, and rich with wellness. She is proud of her body.

Her mind is clear, present and always open. It is at times quiet.

Her spirit shines; shines on those around her and from a place of pure light.

Honoring her body, mind and spirit as one, is important and necessary, and she takes care of all of them, all of the time. Her mind reflects a soft yellow color for inspiration; her body a soft green for rest; and her spirit a rose pink for revitalization.

Seeing a smile from her tells the world around her, and herself, that she is utterly content.

The past has been let go and released from all attachments. The present is fully alive and well. The future is only a concept of time, not a feeling.

This woman carries herself with honor and respect.

She has realized that to love others, she must truly love herself first. So she does.

Promoting forgiveness, this woman has opened her heart to those that have wronged her and releasing. You see, in letting that free, she sets herself free.

She shares wonderful relationships with friends, family and in romance.

There is a powerful love, that which cannot be broken. It flourishes. It is alive and it is beautiful.

Having and living in abundance, giving comes easy. She gives not only monetarily, but she gives her hand. She gives her time, but not without her own time first.

She is one with Father God. One with Mother Earth. One with you.

You see, *she is you*.

Humor

The Lion and the Lamb
Michelle Cheney

The Lion and the Lamb is the tale of March, my birthday, and its moody, wild, windy, dramatic passionate entrance and its gentle loving exit-opening a blossom filled window to warm months.

I live with the Lion and the Lamb. The little lion-glamorous, passionate, determined, bossy, and the sweet lamb- gentle and beautiful, grateful.

Let me tell you first, about my Lion.

She came to me nine years ago, impressing me with a very large bowel movement in an oversized sand box, then, when arriving at my home, jumped into my bed for a nap. She looked like a cartoon version of a weasel, with a long neck, huge ebony ears and face and sky blue eyes. No wonder she was the last one in the litter, the leftover.
But, like March, this little lion grew into a great beauty. A beauty who has presented challenges.

During one of my "moves," I locked this precious feline cargo in the bathroom so she wouldn't escape, but like the late winter wind, she was able to unlock the door with her pussy willow paws and spring herself free. The only way to lasso this wild wind into captivity was with a degrading rabbit cage…much like what you do to the bougainvillea, during a late spring frost.

This little burst of March is immaculate with her litter box. Unless her keeper (me) accidentally shuts the door to her personal lion water closet. Like two months ago, when I was woken to a spring shower on my chest, a reminder that this little lion must be accommodated at all times.

It was a dark February morning when the lion met the lamb. The lamb had been at the Town Lake Animal Shelter, and was delivered to me in a dark parking lot. The terrified, quivering lamb had a little dachshund face, sad brown eyes, and a long efficient waving tail - so efficient, that I questioned the need for air conditioning.

That first morning, as the lamb sat shaking on the kitchen floor, the lion came in, sized up the lamb, and promptly swatted the sweet being across the face. It was clear, that the lion was more fierce than the lamb, but the lamb's gentleness won over the shepherds, and to some degree, the lion.

The lamb lives for her keepers. She stares out the window each day, waiting for the burst of color that comes from those she loves. She sleeps soundly, and like Spring, makes a gentle rumble to remind me that things will change. She loves dinner parties, because of the varied snacks. She is, the promise of love. Always fulfilling, never disappointing.

So I live with the lion and the lamb, a contrast in its simplest and most beautiful form. My Spring has both a lion and a lamb, and that makes me happy.

The Funniest Thing Happened...
The Mother-in-Law
Ann-Marie Fontenot

It's customary in the Muslim countries that I've lived in to have the man possess more than one wife. As a matter of fact, he usually has multiple wives. This is true in the country of Togo, West Africa, where I lived and worked as a Peace Corps Volunteer in the village of Keve for two years. I arrived in Togo at the age of twenty-two, ready to absorb all I could from the rich culture that surrounded me.

One of the first persons I was introduced to in Keve was the Chief of the Village. He graciously welcomed me to his community in my English language; explaining to me that he had learned English as a stowaway on a British ship when he was a boy. What a charming fellow the Chief was! He introduced me to his first wife, a tall, large, and stately figure who always smiled at me. She dressed in colorful pagniers and wore elegant turbans on her head. She was truly regal; and I was drawn to her air of poise and composure. My Chief had other wives, to be sure: eight in total. He also had many children, more than I could count. Over time, I learned that the Muslim man chooses his first wife. Thereafter, she selects his subsequent wives, according to her judgment of their compatibility with herself, as well as their usefulness. With large families of offspring to care for, as well as endless chores of tending gardens, drawing water from the well, cooking, cleaning their huts, washing clothes and cooking utensils, as well as preparing their wares to take to the weekly markets in the neighboring villages (all while being observed by the men sitting comfortably in the shade of a nearby coffee bean tree), these women need each other for companionship and mutual support in maintaining a household.

Once settled into my village, the Chief and I established a delightful routine of enjoying afternoon tea at his compound. Afternoon tea was a custom that the Chief had adopted while he was in England as a young man. We conversed in English, which the Chief enjoyed practicing and I found relaxing as a respite from the French language and EWE dialect that the villagers spoke. The Chief described his dreams for his village; and we discussed my role in helping him accomplish his goals. A particularly important project that the Chief hoped to establish in his village of Keve was to build a hospital. He asked me if I could secure funds with which to build a local hospital. I successfully applied to the American Embassy for a grant to build a two-bedroom hospital in Keve. Later, I received U.S. funds with which to lay a new roof over the village school. The Chief was very pleased with my work.

On one momentousness afternoon, the Chief informed me that his first wife approved of me. He then asked me if I would be the Chief's ninth wife? Amused at first, I respectfully answered that I would consider it and let him know in time. I thought about the opportunity that wedding the Village Chief would grant me: why, I would be Chieftess of my village . . . that is, after the first, second, third, fourth, fifth, sixth, seventh, and eighth wife, I would be Chieftess of the village! I saw my future expanding!

In the meantime, I continued my work as a lowly Peace Corps Volunteer: I taught Preventative Health in the village clinics and Health lessons in the elementary schools in Keve and in three other villages that I traveled to by motorcycle, as they were situated in the "bush," away from any public road. All proceeded well during my stay in Keve. That is, until Kathy, the new Peace Corps Volunteer, moved into Assahoun, the village just up the road from Keve. Kathy was of Swedish descent: she was big, heavy-set, tall, and blond. She had more of everything than I could ever hope to have.

It's customary for Peace Corps Volunteers to visit at each others' houses during the week-ends, for companionship. Many Saturdays, I rode my motorcycle up the dirt road to Assahoun to visit Kathy for the night or she would ride her motorcycle down to Keve to spend the night with me. One week-end afternoon, I made the mistake of bringing Kathy to tea with me to introduce her to my Chief.

I was unsuspecting of the enamourment that my Chief would succumb to upon seeing my blond, wellendowed friend. To my chagrin, I learned weeks later that, from that fatal day forward, Kathy and my Chief began enjoying afternoon tea alone – without me! The day arrived when my Chief announced to me, "Ann-Marie, never mind about you being my ninth wife; Kathy will be my ninth wife." "You can be the Mother-in-Law."

With Mother-in-Law resignation, I handed Kathy to my Chief, bestowing upon them my blessings and relinquishing once and forever my dream of being Chieftess (that is, ninth Chieftess) of the village. With a nod to the new couple, I swung my leg over my motorcycle and rode off into the sunset...

www.ingramcontent.com/pod-product-compliance
Lightning Source LLC
Chambersburg PA
CBHW052041280426
43661CB00084B/7